SMALL WORLD

Meet **30** of Earth's Tiniest Creatures

Written by **NICK CRUMPTON**

Illustrated by **ROSIE DORE**

SMALL WORLD © 2025 Quarto Publishing plc.
Text © 2025 Nick Crumpton. Illustrations © 2025 Rosie Dore.

First Published in 2025 by Wide Eyed Editions,
an imprint of The Quarto Group.
100 Cummings Center, Suite 255D, Beverly, MA 01915, USA.
T +1 978-282-9590 www.Quarto.com

The right of Nick Crumpton to be identified as the author and Rosie Dore to be identified as the illustrator of this work has been asserted by them in accordance with the Copyright, Designs and Patents Act, 1988 (United Kingdom).

All rights reserved.

No part of this publication may be reproduced, stored in a retrieval system, or transmitted, in any form, or by any means, electrical, mechanical, photocopying, recording or otherwise without the prior written permission of the publisher or a licence permitting restricted copying.

ISBN 978-0-7112-8857-7

The illustrations were created digitally.
Set in BuenaParkJF, Quasimoda and Mrs Eaves OT

Designer: Lyli Feng and Kathryn Davies
Commissioning Editor: Hannah Dove
Editor: Hannah Dove
Production Controller: Robin Boothroyd
Art Director: Karissa Santos
Publisher: Georgia Buckthorn

Manufactured in Guangdong, China CC122024

9 8 7 6 5 4 3 2 1

Written by NICK CRUMPTON   Illustrated by ROSIE DORE

SMALL WORLD

Meet 30 of Earth's Tiniest Creatures

WIDE EYED EDITIONS

CONTENTS

6-7 INTRODUCTION

8-9 BIRDS
- 10-11 Bee hummingbird
- 12-13 Black-thighed falconet
- 14-15 Goldcrest
- 16-17 Elf owl
- 18-19 Australian little penguin
- 20-21 Life-size birds

22-23 FISH
- 24-25 Mini carp
- 26-27 Denise's pygmy seahorse
- 28-29 Dwarf lantern shark
- 30-31 Male fanfin angler
- 32-33 Ocellaris clownfish
- 34-35 Life-size fish

36-37 AMPHIBIANS
- 38-39 Broad-snout casque-headed tree frog
- 40-41 Olm
- 42-43 Taita Hills caecilian
- 44-45 Oak toad
- 46-47 Pumpkin toadlet
- 48-49 Life-size amphibians

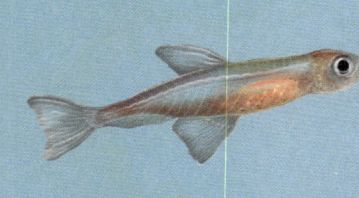

50–51 INVERTEBRATES

52–53 Monarch butterfly
54–55 Coconut octopus
56–57 Common kingslayer
58–59 Pom-pom crab
60–61 Peacock spider
62–63 Life-size invertebrates

64–65 MAMMALS

66–67 Hero shrew
68–69 Kitti's hog-nosed bat
70–71 Fennec fox
72–73 Rusty-spotted cat
74–75 Western pygmy marmoset
76–77 Life-size mammals

78–79 REPTILES

80–81 Nano-chameleon
82–83 Armadillo lizard
84–85 Speckled Cape tortoise
86–87 Barbados threadsnake
88–89 Indian flying lizard
90–91 Life-size reptiles

92–93 THE VERY SMALLEST ANIMALS

94–95 GLOSSARY
96 INDEX

INTRODUCTION

Our world is big.

Towering mountains climb up into a vast sky.
Huge waves crash against immense coastlines.
Massive sand dunes blow across great deserts.
Wide rivers wind through thick, far-reaching forests.
Giant beasts roam, soar, and swim.

But the story doesn't end there . . .

In every corner of nature, from pools, hedges, and caves, to streams, treetops, and sandy deserts, Earth's tiniest inhabitants go about their lives. They avoid monstrous predators and conquer colossal landscapes, all the while trying to find food and shelter, attract mates, and raise their young.

From the humid undergrowth of the Amazon rainforest to the branches of the smallest coral in the ocean, tiny animals have adapted to thrive, despite—and sometimes because of—their size.

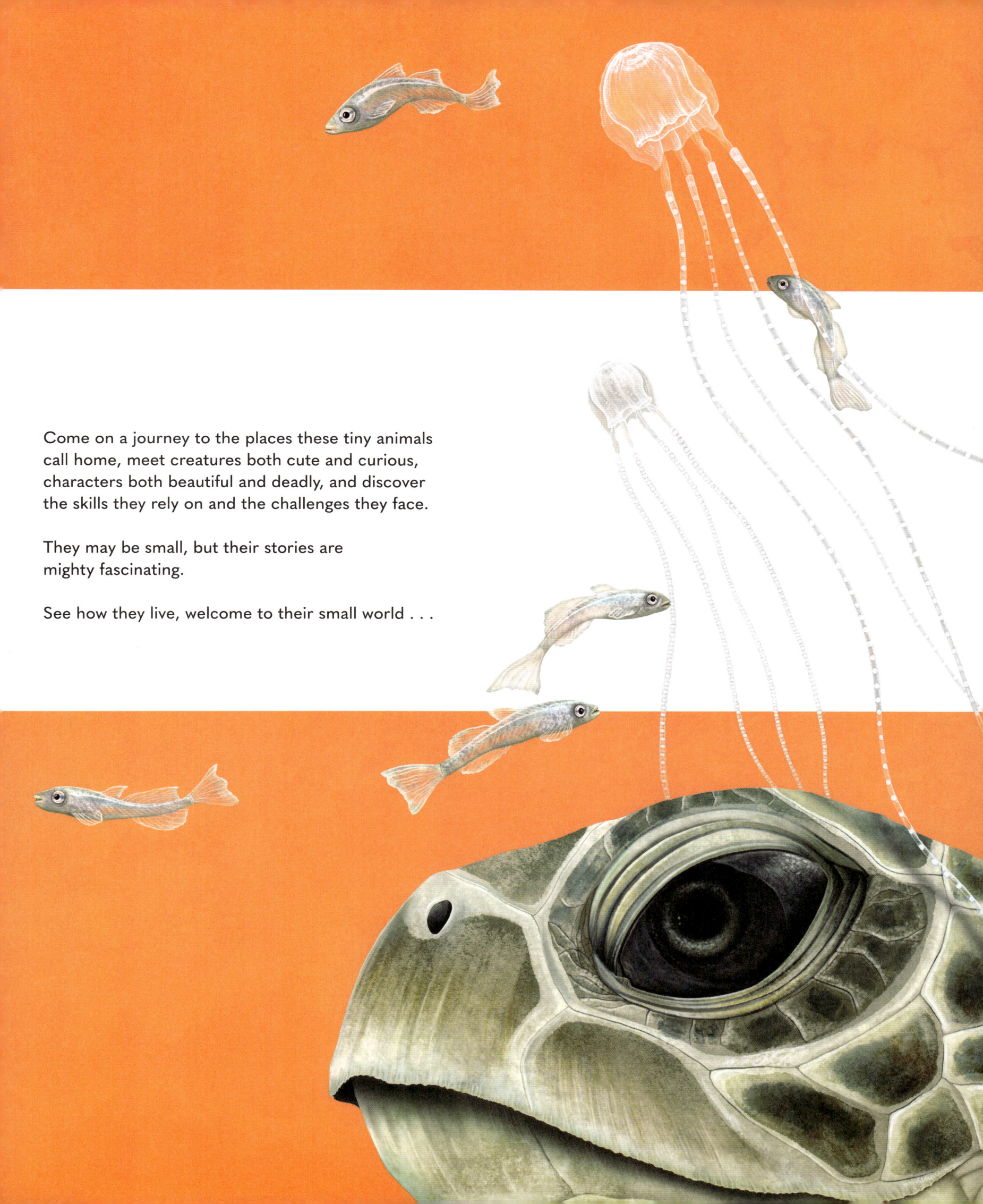

Come on a journey to the places these tiny animals call home, meet creatures both cute and curious, characters both beautiful and deadly, and discover the skills they rely on and the challenges they face.

They may be small, but their stories are mighty fascinating.

See how they live, welcome to their small world . . .

BIRDS

From robins to eagles and coots to cranes, the thousands of species of birds that fill up our skies today are what's left of the dinosaurs that once roamed Earth. Through millions of years of evolution, these masters of the air are now found almost everywhere on the planet. Though many of their ancestors from the Jurassic and Cretaceous periods reached enormous sizes, the heavier a bird is, the trickier it is to remain in the air, so it helps to be small if you want to fly.

Today, our skies are filled with many species of spectacular small birds. They hide in branches and abandoned crannies in walls and trees to avoid hungry predators. But using their feathered wings requires lots of energy. So while these tiny birds might be small, they have humongous appetites and they do everything they can to save as much energy as possible.

Bee hummingbird

Mellisuga helenae

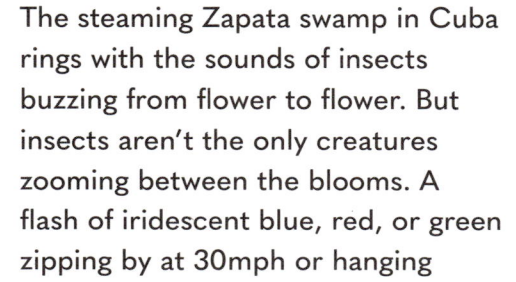

The steaming Zapata swamp in Cuba rings with the sounds of insects buzzing from flower to flower. But insects aren't the only creatures zooming between the blooms. A flash of iridescent blue, red, or green zipping by at 30mph or hanging motionless in the air might look like a beautiful bee, but it's actually the smallest bird in the world: the bee hummingbird.

Birds are all very light for their size thanks to their hollow bones, and this

Bee hummingbirds are fast fliers. They can beat their wings up to an incredible 200 times every second, which requires a lot of energy. The most energy-rich food for an animal this size is nectar: the sugary, sticky liquid produced by flowers that keeps the hummingbird's body going.

These tiny birds are almost always hungry and can eat half their body weight in nectar per day, slurping it up with their tongue as they hold themselves still in mid-air. As they visit more than 1,000 flowers each day, they move pollen from one flower to another, helping pollinate them so they can create the next generation of plants. These teensy birds help nature to thrive.

2 inch-long acrobat weighs only 2g. You would barely feel it if it landed on the back of your hand. These birds prefer their own company, only meeting up when it's time to find a mate. Red-throated males will group together and sing to win over the females. Instead of using branches or sticks to build their nests, bee hummingbirds use small pieces of bark and moss, stuck together with spiders' webs to protect their eggs—which are only the size of baked beans. Their chicks hatch after only 21 days and are ready to fly just two weeks after that (which is handy when there are hungry spiders and frogs on your trail!).

Black-thighed falconet

Microhierax fringillarius

Raptors (or birds of prey) are usually thought of as majestic predators: imposing hunters soaring on the wind, coasting on vast, outstretched wings. But flitting above the rice fields of Borneo, diving swiftly off and back to their perches, one of the world's smallest birds of prey looks a lot more like a scruffy black and white parrot than an elegant hawk.

The fact that they look a bit like parrots isn't that strange. Falcons, such as the black-thighed falconet, are actually more closely related to parrots and perching birds like robins and blackbirds than they are to eagles, hawks, and owls.

Having such a small wingspan (about 11 inches) helps the black-thighed falconet twist and turn much quicker in the air than its larger relatives. This means it can fly after—and catch—some of the most agile, zippiest prey. Being small is an advantage for this plucky predator.

Rather than hunting large prey like other birds, black-thighed falconets focus their binocular vision and aim their tearing beaks at small land-prey such as lizards, and even smaller aerial snacks, like butterflies and dragonflies (although they have occasionally been seen killing larger birds such as babblers).

Unlike other raptors, falconets seem to like hunting together in teams of up to ten, perching next to each other on tree branches and jumping off in turn to quickly snatch insects from the air. This is a hunting style called "sallying."

Being so small, it makes sense to save energy where you can—like when it comes to building nests. Instead of making their own, clever black-thighed falconets reuse old barbet or woodpecker holes that aren't being used by their original creators anymore.

Black-thighed falconets might look sweet, but their incredible agility, fast flight, and sharp eyesight make them impressive hunters of the insects and smaller animals they share their environment with.

Goldcrest

Regulus regulus

Deep in any cool-scented **coniferous** forest in the UK, you're likely to hear the trilling whistle of the goldcrest. Both the males and the females of these tiny, round, perching birds have a browny-green body and head. The females are crowned with a bright yellow stripe, while the males have a fiery orange stripe. At only 3.5 inches long, and with a tiny 5.5 inch wingspan, they are the smallest birds found in the UK, but that stunning yellow coloration makes them easy to spot.

The goldcrest sings while it forages, constantly moving in twitchy hops along the branches of trees like spruce or Scots pine

Goldcrests may be common in the UK right now, but they rely on their conifer forest homes to survive. They can't live anywhere else. This means, these tiny feathered fliers need their habitat to be respected and protected so they can continue ruling royally.

looking for insects, often balancing on single pine tree needles as it hunts.

Its slender beak is excellently adapted for nipping in the narrow gaps between needles for minute prey such as springtails, small spiders, and insects with soft, easy-to-eat exoskeletons like caterpillars. But sometimes it steals insects trapped in spiders' webs before the spiders can get to them.

The bright yellow or orange "crown" of feathers gives the goldcrest its scientific name *Regulus regulus*, which means "little king." For humans, crowns are displays of power and importance—and it's the same for goldcrests. Males looking to attract mates bow their heads and raise and fan out their bright orange feathers like a brilliant flame.

Goldcrests, like other small birds, have to look out for merlins—the UK's smallest raptor— as well as sparrowhawks and owls. Luckily, goldcrests' incredibly small size make them a very difficult prey to catch, especially when they move through the woodland with their bouncing, erratic flight, which helps protect them.

While adult elf owls have to look out for predators, their tiny chicks have smaller dangers to worry about: parasites and meat-eating insects that can creep into their homes. To protect their chicks, elf owls capture threadsnakes and drop them in the abandoned woodpecker holes they use for nests in saguaro cacti. The threadsnakes act as housekeepers, keeping the nest free of pests by snapping them up in their miniature jaws.

Elf owl
Micrathene whitneyi

Over a canyon road at dusk somewhere in the Baja California Peninsula, silent, ghostly forms swoop bat-like through the thick, warm air, or silhouetted against the purple sky. Standing at just 6 inches tall, you could hold this creature in the palm of your hand (and at less than the weight of a golf ball, you wouldn't get a sore arm).

Being so small, elf owls hunt equally tiny prey: occasionally little mammals such as kangaroo rats, but more often insects such as moths. As these nocturnal insects are drawn to sources of light, elf owls like to hang out around streetlights, where they can swoop in and catch their fluttering dinner on the wing.

There's safety in numbers, and when elf owls spot danger in the form of snakes—or bigger owls—they work together to dive and swoop at possible predators to scare them away. Although there's nothing particularly intimidating about a single elf owl, a parliament (the name for a group of owls) of them can cause a scare!

If elf owls *are* caught by a predator, their diminutive size means they can't fight to protect themselves. Instead, they pretend to be dead. As soon as the predator thinks it no longer has to hold on to its prize, the crafty owl jumps up and makes its escape!

Australian little penguin

Eudyptula novaehollandiae

Penguins might conjure up images of epic icy landscapes, blistering winds, and a life of hardship at the edges of the Earth, but not all of these handsome aquatic birds live in such extremes. The Australian little penguin (sometimes called 'the blue penguin' because of its magnificently colored plumage , and sometimes called 'the fairy penguin' because of its adorable size) is one such penguin that lives a little closer to our human world.

At only 12 inches tall (you'd need to stand three on top of each other to reach the height of their Antarctic cousin, the Emperor penguin), these penguins are the tiniest of all penguin species and live in coastal regions along the shores of Southern Australia.

Although they spend nearly all day miles out at sea hunting crustaceans, squid, and jellyfish, and sometimes spend weeks eating and sleeping on the waves, they return to the shore during the Southern Hemisphere's winter to dig sandy burrows and find mates in colonies.

Males and females get to know each other by performing courting rituals. The male penguin first attracts a female by holding his head up and calling. (Despite their size, these teeny birds are known for being noisy!) When a female is interested, she stands across from her suitor. They each have their flippers held outstretched, and together they walk around the burrow nest in tight circles in a wonderful love dance.

The biggest threats to little penguins are animals that have been introduced to Australia since European humans arrived (such as dogs, cats and foxes), because the tiny birds haven't evolved to exist alongside them.

Many species around the world that are facing extinction are in this predicament because they are at risk of being eaten—or being beaten to finding food—by animals that have been introduced by humans, including dogs, cats, rats, and goats. Although humans can create these problems, we can also solve them: in Warrnambool, Australia, humans managed to help protect little penguins from these "introduced" predators by stationing trained Maremma sheepdogs as guards around the colony to frighten off foxes and feral pets, giving these little penguins a better chance to survive and thrive.

As well as threats from non-native animals, little penguins face other dangers. Their tiny chicks might be eaten by large predators such as sea eagles and monitor lizards.

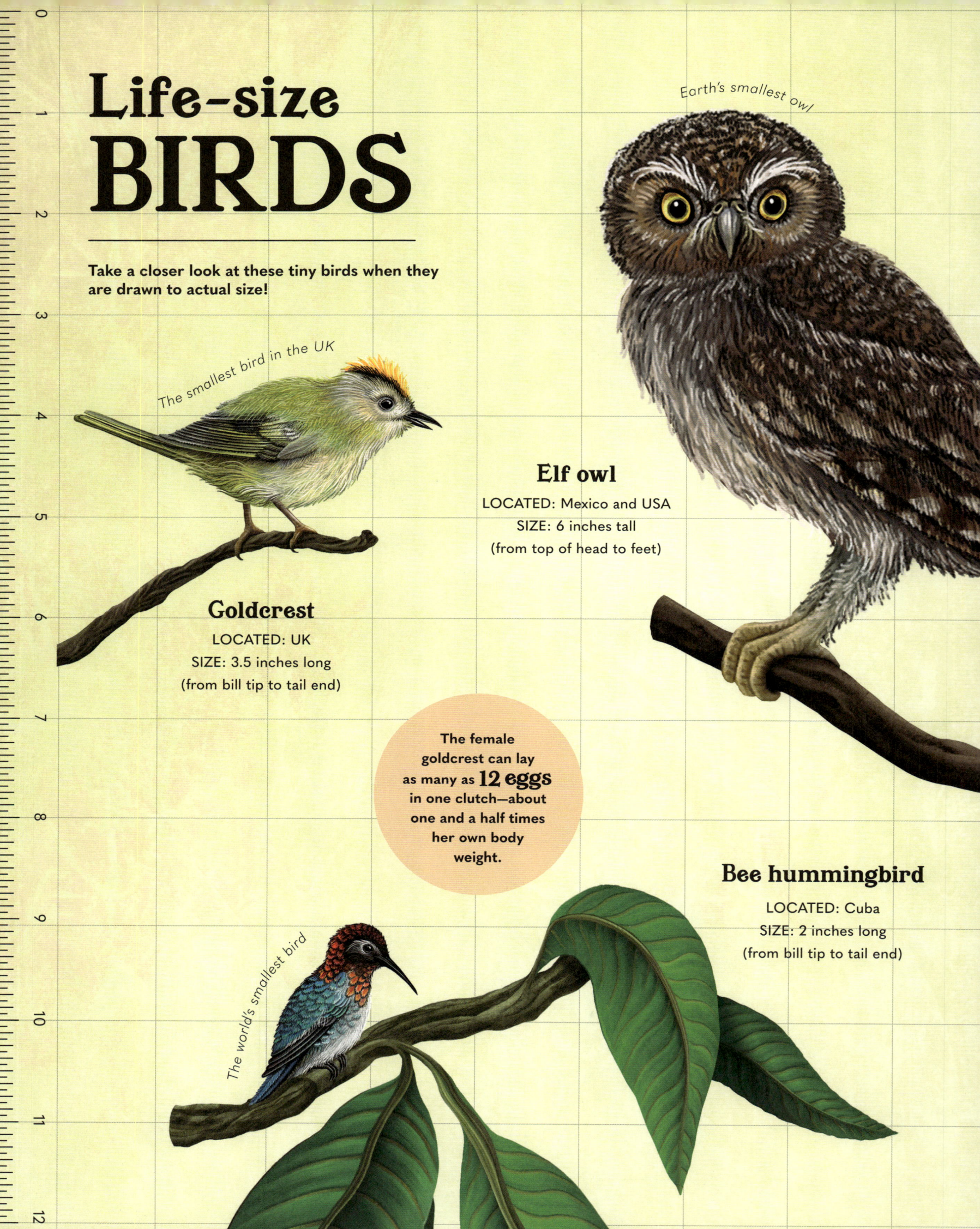

Life-size BIRDS

Take a closer look at these tiny birds when they are drawn to actual size!

Earth's smallest owl

The smallest bird in the UK

Elf owl
LOCATED: Mexico and USA
SIZE: 6 inches tall
(from top of head to feet)

Goldcrest
LOCATED: UK
SIZE: 3.5 inches long
(from bill tip to tail end)

The female goldcrest can lay as many as **12 eggs** in one clutch—about one and a half times her own body weight.

Bee hummingbird
LOCATED: Cuba
SIZE: 2 inches long
(from bill tip to tail end)

The world's smallest bird

The smallest penguin species

Australian little penguin

LOCATED: Australia and New Zealand
SIZE: 12 inches tall

Australian little penguins can make a big noise, especially when they return to their nesting sites at dusk. What's more, they speak with a different "accent" to closely related penguins in New Zealand!

Earth's smallest bird of prey

Black-thighed falconet

LOCATED: Malaysia, Indonesia, Brunei, Myanmar, Thailand, and Singapore
SIZE: 6 inches long
(from bill tip to tail end)

FISH

Animals need to find things—food to eat, other animals to mate with, and places to shelter or lay eggs, for example. They also need to look out for danger from other creatures that might want to fight them for territory, or worse, eat them. Most animals on land have to look (and look *out*) for these things in a two-dimensional world—forward and backward and left and right. Some animals have to look up as well, to be on the look-out for predators on the wing, and a few have to think about what's below them—if they swing around in trees. But fish live in a truly three-dimensional world, where fresh or salt water can stretch away from them in front and behind, and away from each of their sides. But, balancing in the water, both opportunity and danger can be found above them toward the shining surface and below them, toward the gloom of the seabed. It's a vast, dark world down there—and finding things being found, and making yourself invisible, are constant challenges to the world's smallest fish.

Mini carp

Paedocypris progenetica

Within the rivers flowing through the peat swamps of Sumatra and the Bintan islands of Indonesia, almost invisible movements catch the dim light just above the riverbed. As the plants clogging the water grow, die, and rot, chemicals called tannins seep out into the river, staining it like a cup of tea. Only a few species can survive in this slightly acidic environment, and one of these animals is very, very small.

For a while, *Paedocypris* was thought to be the smallest vertebrate in the world (actually, that record-holder is now thought to be a tiny frog), but you'd still be hard pressed to spot one of these tiny 8mm-long fish—especially in the dark water they hide in.

It's almost impossible to have a skeleton and be smaller than *Paedocypris*. In fact, to be this small, lots of parts of its skeleton can't even grow as they would in larger fish.

Like many other fish, **Paedocypris** live in groups called schools to protect themselves from predators such as aquatic beetles and dragonfly larvae.

Its brain, for instance, isn't completely protected by its skull bones, because the bones can't quite lock together as they do in bigger fish.

Their transparent bodies also make it much harder to see *Paedocypris* in the gloomy water. Only when they are observed under bright lights by scientists do their tail muscles and other features stand out as colorful structures.

Being this small is helpful for an animal that lives in an environment that can sometimes dry out—even if its home is reduced to the size of a puddle, this tiny member of the carp family can still survive until more rains arrive. But living in such a *specific* place can be dangerous. The less able you are to live in other places, the more likely you are to go extinct if your habitat gets destroyed. This miniature fish was only described in 2006, but sadly scientists know its populations are already decreasing because of threats to its home, such as logging and palm oil farming.

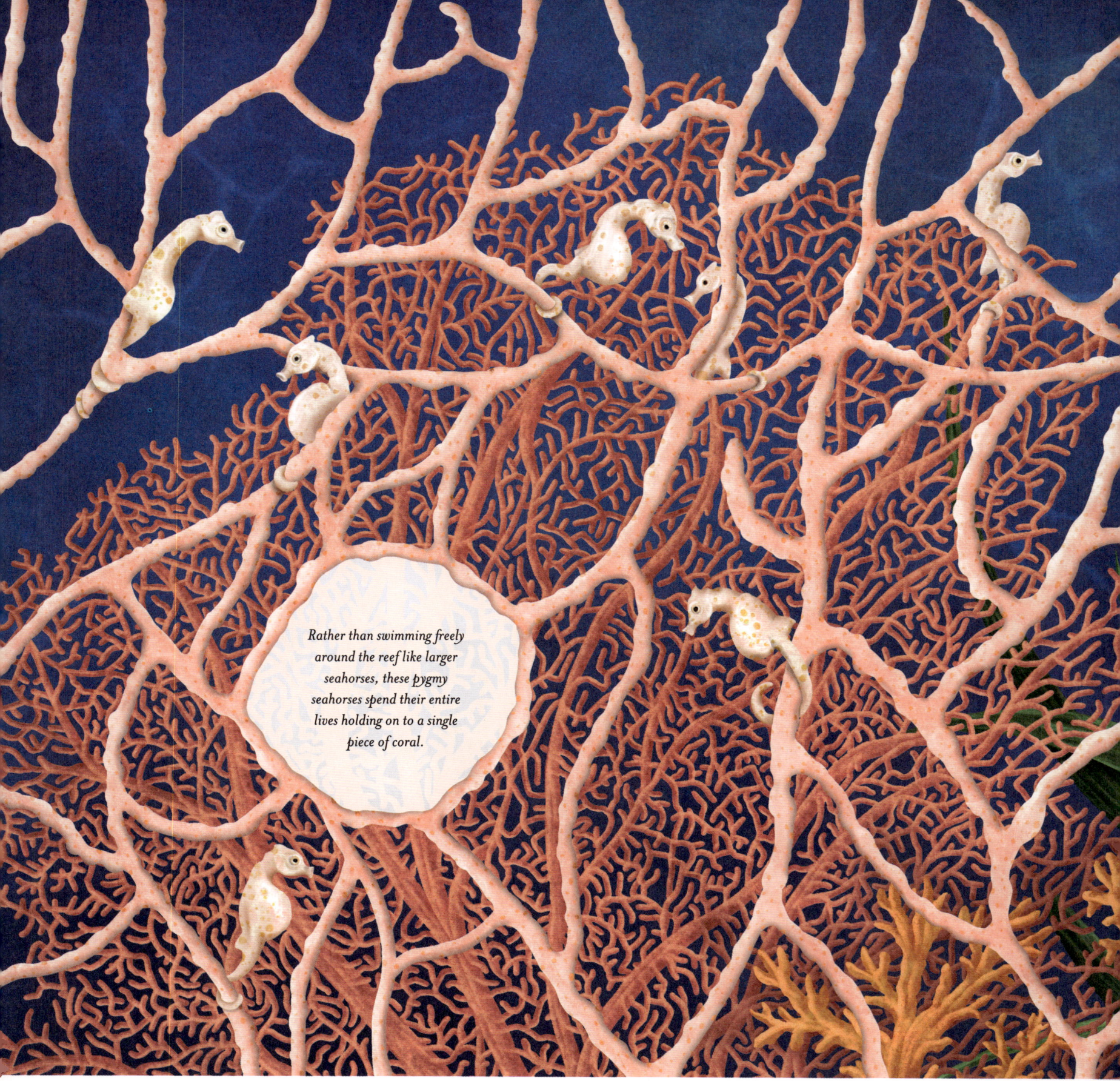

Rather than swimming freely around the reef like larger seahorses, these pygmy seahorses spend their entire lives holding on to a single piece of coral.

Denise's pygmy seahorse

Hippocampus denise

Diving above coral reefs in the warm, shallow seas off the coasts of Indonesia, you might spot some beautiful sharks, vibrant sea slugs, even some colorful jellyfish. But if you look closely—very, *very* closely—at the branches of sea fan corals, you *might* just be able to spot one of the smallest fish in the ocean: a Denise's pygmy seahorse.

Two adult Denise's pygmy seahorses may look like completely different types of fish. Like other seahorses, baby Denise's pygmy seahorses are born from their fathers, not their mothers. After they arrive as a baby fish at the coral that will be their lifelong home, they change the color and texture of their skin within just a few days to look identical

Because pygmy seahorses are so small and so incredible at camouflaging themselves, scientists have only known about them for about 50 years. Denise's pygmy seahorses were only discovered in 1999 when scientist Sara Lourie spotted the species with marine photographer Denise Tackett, after whom this particular seahorse is named.

to their new surroundings. They are masters of disguise—a handy trick when you are surrounded by hungry giants such as rays.

Dwarf lantern shark

Etmopterus perryi

About 1,300 feet below the surface of the ocean, off the coast of Colombia in South America, our human eyes would hardly be able to see a thing in the almost pitch-black deep. And yet, if we looked hard enough, we might think we saw barely visible flashes of pale light moving through the water, but then they disappear . . . hidden in the gloom. Maybe, just maybe, we saw a dwarf lantern shark calling and luring its prey.

Dwarf lantern sharks are the smallest sharks humans know about in the oceans, only reaching a maximum length of about 8 inches. But these little sharks have lots of interesting features.

The sharks' photophores may also help them find and communicate with other members of their species in such low light. Once they have found each other, and after the sharks mate, female dwarf lantern sharks give birth to tiny live young, rather than laying egg cases.

Only 1% of light from the surface of the ocean manages to reach such great depths—the so-called twilight zone. In order to make the most of such a miniscule amount of light, dwarf lantern sharks have enormous eyes relative to the length of their bodies.

Being so small in such impenetrable gloom, dwarf lantern sharks might find it almost impossible to find prey to eat—so instead, they use an amazing adaptation to attract animals straight to them. On the underside of their bodies, as well as on their fins, are bioluminescent "photophores," special areas of their skin that generate light. It's very likely these lights attract curious fish, which the lantern sharks can then snap up in their toothy jaws.

Another way lantern sharks can use their lights is to make themselves invisible. In the same way that some larger sharks have paler undersides to help them look lighter against the bright water surface when viewed from below, the dwarf lantern shark's lights can match the small amount of light reaching the twilight zone. This makes them disappear when seen from below, rather than appearing as a darker silhouette against the dimly lit upper water. All the better to sneak and pounce with!

Male fanfins rely on their large eyes and big nostrils to find females in the inky dark waters.

Male fanfin angler

Caulophryne jordani

In the deep depths of the ocean, 2,600 feet below the surface off the coast of the Azores Islands, an 8 inch-long, ball-shaped fish hangs almost motionless in the frigid water. The female fanfin angler is surrounded by a wispy curtain of slender filaments helping it sense anything in the water that might be worth investigating.

Female fanfins, like other anglerfish, use bioluminescent "lures"—fleshy parts of their bodies on stalks—to attract prey to eat, convincing their victims that they're investigating a tasty-looking snack, before snapping them up.

Finding a mate in the darkness can be a problem, but anglerfish such as the fanfin

Because it's so unlikely a male anglerfish sniffs out pheromones in the first place and then actually manages to track a female down in this perpetual darkness, this "parasitic" mating means they both never have to worry about looking for another hard-to-find mate ever again.

have evolved an amazing solution. The females release a chemical signal called a pheromone that males can follow like a trail. Then, when one finds her, he grabs hold of her skin in his jaws . . . and never lets go—like a fishy hitchhiker!

Anglerfish are very difficult for humans to study because their bodies break down easily when they are taken up out of the high pressure of the deep ocean. But when these fish are accidentally brought up into our world, they are always the larger females—together with one small male (or more) hanging on.

The males are tiny at around 0.6 inches in length—much, much smaller than the females—and as they hold on, their heads slowly become fused to the female and their bodies begin to work as one— even sharing a circulatory system. Over time, a male's eyes, intestines, gills, all disappear as he becomes one with his mate.

Ocellaris clownfish

Amphiprion ocellaris

In and around the brown and green mass of giant carpet anemones, a group of familiar small fish weaves in and out of the finger-like tentacles, buffeted around in the shallow ocean currents surrounding the Philippines. A deep orange, chunky fish with white stripes outlined by black ridges, Ocellaris clownfish—or anemonefish—make their home in and among their venomous partner.

Ocellaris clownfish usually grow to around 3–4.5 inches long, and they are much smaller than this when they first descend from the surface of the sea as young fish to pick an anemone to live in.

Clownfish wear a thick layer of clear mucus over their body. Just as mucus protects the sensitive inside of your nose from being irritated by things you breathe in, clownfish mucus protects the fish from being stung by the anemone, so they can hide deep in the tentacles where larger, unprotected fish such as eels can't reach them.

Although they are small, clownfish have a serious temper and defend their homes from any other fish that try to move in with a bad attitude, biting and chasing the intruder away.

Ocellaris clownfish live with others in a "society" with very strict layers of importance, or "dominance." There is usually just one female in the group, who is the largest, and she gets the biggest share of food. The smallest fish nibble on any scraps left behind.

If the female dies or leaves, the largest male takes her place, turning into a female. Instead of waiting for a new, small female to choose the anemone, this means the group can keep making baby fish right away, ensuring more and more generations of teeny-tiny clownfish.

Life-size FISH

Take a closer look at these tiny fish when they are drawn to actual size!

Mini carp
LOCATED: Peat swamps and blackwater streams in Indonesia
SIZE: 8 mm long

The world's smallest fish

Ocellaris clownfish
LOCATED: Indian and Pacific Oceans
SIZE: 3–4.5 inches long

Small but spirited, this feisty fish defends its anemone home

The female ocellaris clownfish can lay up to **1,000 tiny** (3–4mm) orange eggs. The male then tends them until they hatch.

Denise's pygmy seahorse
LOCATED: Pacific Ocean
SIZE: They range in length from 0.5–1 inch (between the tip of the tail to the end of the snout)

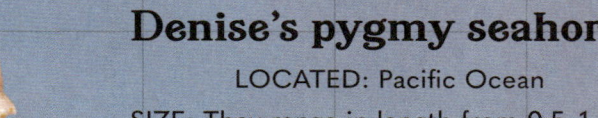

The smallest seahorse

The smallest shark in the ocean

Dwarf lantern shark
LOCATED: Caribbean Sea
SIZE: 8 inches long (maximum size for female)

Humans have explored and charted a tiny 5% of Earth's ocean. How many super-small species might be hiding in its depths?

The tiny male is a "parasitic" partner to the much larger female

Fanfin angler

LOCATED: Atlantic, Indian and Pacific Oceans
SIZE: 8 inches long for the female
0.6 inches long for the male

AMPHIBIANS

Most amphibians are small, but some are really, *really* small—which means they're usually on something else's menu. Unlike many other animals that live on the land, amphibians can't run or fly away anywhere to escape danger—they need to stay connected to water to feed, lay eggs, and even breathe! Amphibians get around this thanks to some incredible adaptations and behavior, like living in hard-to-reach underground flooded caves, or living most of their lives buried under moist soil. But if you have to live on the surface, you can always make yourself very brightly colored and taste really terrible—even *poisonous.* It's a frog-eat-frog world out there, and if you're bite-sized, it pays to have some tricks up your sleeves.

37

Broad-snout casque-headed tree frog

Aparasphenodon arapapa

A few feet above the Brazilian Atlantic Forest floor, surrounded by cascades of thick green leaves and splashes of floral color, a male broad-snout casque-headed tree frog lies completely still, invisible to any animal passing by. Although it might not look like it, he is caring for his young, and like all other members of his species, he relies on only a few of the 10,000 species of plants that grow here and nowhere else on Earth to guarantee his young's survival.

Amphibians can't make hard eggshells like reptiles and birds can to stop their eggs from drying out. Instead they have to lay their soft eggs in water for their

Lots of small animals have large numbers of predators to protect their young from and some, including the broad-snout casque-headed tree frog, go to extremes—like using their own bodies as defenses—to keep their next generation from danger. Brave little frogs!

young to grow properly. This isn't a problem if you live near a river or pond, but broad-snout casque-headed tree frogs tend to live in the middle of forests far away from these water sources.

Instead, these tiny 2.5 inch-long frogs use the rainwater collected inside circles of leaves (called rosettes) in bromeliad plants that grow throughout South America as miniature water-nurseries, laying their eggs into these handy pocket-sized puddles.

After the eggs are laid by the female, the male frog stays in the leafy lagoon (or, to use the scientific word, *phytotelmata*) for three weeks while their tadpoles grow into frogs. The tadpoles can't move from one bromeliad to another and have no defences if they are discovered. To protect them while they are so helpless, the male uses his bony, wedge-shaped head as a trap door to the pool, sealing it off from any predators.

Although it might sound like a good idea to use the biggest bromeliads as a home for tadpoles to grow bigger, broad-snout casque-headed tree frogs need to find rosettes with perfect, frog-sized pools so their heads can form a tight seal. If the plant is too big, the frog's head won't be able to cover the whole pool, and predators can more easily slip in through any gaps down into the nursery below.

Olm

Proteus anguinus

It is not unusual to find salamanders in and around water: they are amphibians, so they need to stay damp to make sure their skin doesn't dry out. However, it is unusual to find salamanders in pitch black, underground flooded caves. But that's exactly where the 9.5 inch-long, ghostly white olm lives: deep beneath the Dinarides Alps in Southern Europe.

These slender salamanders live their entire lives in complete darkness, filtering tiny prey such as shrimp from the water through their teeth. They only need to catch a small amount to eat, because food is so hard to come by in this environment, they have evolved to survive for long amounts of time—up to ten years—between meals.

Unlike most other amphibians, olms don't go through metamorphosis or become terrestrial as adults. Instead, they spend their lives underwater, in a juvenile-like state, breathing through their feathery gills, like tadpoles.

Olms have no pigment in their pale skin, making them appear very bright when taken above ground by curious scientists. Under sunlight, their paleness would make them targets for larger predators or obvious to their prey but since no light penetrates into their subterranean homes, olms don't need to worry about hiding from their prey; animals only need to be camouflaged if there's the risk of being seen . . .

Living in complete darkness, olms have lost the use of their eyes, which are covered over with skin. Instead of vision, they rely on sensing smells, movement, and the electric fields of other animals to find their way through their underground lakes.

41

Taita Hills caecilian

Boulengerula taitana

On a forest floor around the edges of the Taita Hills in Kenya, the ground is moving. The damp soil bulges and parts, revealing a smooth head, smaller than a human fingertip. She tastes the air with a sensitive tentacle beneath her eye, and returns back under the ground. Covered in light colored rings and lacking arms or legs, she may have looked like an earthworm, but this was no invertebrate. She was an amphibian: a Taita Hills caecilian.

It's unusual for an amphibian not to have legs, but for this teeny creature it's a great strategy for getting around. Although it's hard to tell from the outside, Taita Hills caecilians' tails are actually very short—if they did have legs, they'd be right at the very end of their 12 inch-long bodies.

Caecilians are predators and hunt termites, ants, and even venomous centipedes. To crunch through those invertebrate exoskeletons, they rely on not one but two rows of sharp teeth, housed within a sturdy skull which is fused together to withstand pushing through the ground headfirst.

Female Taita Hills caecilians stay underground to care for their young, which are laid as eggs in a subterranean chamber and protected by their mother until they push their way out of their soft eggs. Instead of risking her and her young's safety by venturing onto the surface to hunt, the mother provides food and nutrients in a selfless manner: she lets her young climb on top of her and eat her skin! She has grown a nutritious layer that her tiny-mouthed babies can nibble off, providing them with moisture and nourishment without any of them having to leave their den.

Offering yourself up as a meal to your babies is just one of the amazing adaptations of these mini miners. Although over 200 species of caecilians are known, it is likely there are many more to discover, each with their own evolutionary solutions to living life in a big world.

Only when the warm rains of spring begin to fall do oak toads venture out onto the surface more often. Males climb out of their burrows, fill up their throat sacs, and sing to let females know exactly where they are.

Oak toad
Anaxyrus quercicus

It's humid down on the Florida coast in the USA, and the air hums with tens of thousands of insects: a perfect place to be an amphibian. And it is here, pushing aside the loose surface soil of a steaming forest, that North America's easiest-to-miss toad calls home.

Thirty-three different species of frogs and toads live in Florida, but most of them are much bigger than this one. Oak toads are no larger than a coin (only 0.8–1.2 inches), but the bright stripe on their backs would make them stand out on the forest floor. Their striking coloring isn't often seen though, because oak toads have a habit of burying themselves under soil for most of the year.

Oak toads are voracious hunters of ants, but they have more than their fair share of predators to look out for. Hognose snakes pose a particular threat, but so too do enemies closer to home: larger frogs and toads!

When finding themselves snout to snout with danger, oak toads do what small toads do best: make themselves look bigger, and smell and taste awful. By swallowing air, the toad inflates itself like a miniature balloon, and then releases toxins from its skin to make its newly bloated body even less appetizing-looking to would-be toad-tasters.

Pumpkin toadlet

Brachycephalus ephippium

Beside a gurgling stream cutting a path through the otherwise impenetrable rainforest of Southeast Brazil, the brown and green leaves littering the ground are decorated with tiny blobs of color, brightening up the dim world kept in shadow by thousands of towering trees. Each blob is defending its territory, singing out despite the din of the water. They are pumpkin toadlets, one of the smallest frogs in the world— and one of the smallest animals with a backbone. They're barely longer than 1cm from the tip of their nose to their bottom.

They may be small in size, but pumpkin toadlets are big in color. Their skin is a vivid orange, and a classic case of "aposematic coloration" where animals are brightly colored to tell other animals just how dangerous they are to eat. And dangerous they are: their skin and internal organs are highly toxic and can cause paralysis in any predator unwise enough to try a nibble.

Although adults show off to the rest of the forest with their bright skin, young toadlets are camouflaged to match the forest floor. They need to be well hidden from any possible predators because they can't rely on hiding as tadpoles in a cozy and safe pool—they hatch out of their eggs as fully formed (very small) baby toadlets.

The toadlets are so small their organs of balance (their inner ears) don't work very well and tend to spin out of control if they attempt to jump! The sound-receiving part of their ears don't seem to function well at this small size either. Although they can croak, they can't actually hear the calls of their own species.

A bright orange toadlet that sings but can't hear, can jump but can't land, and that isn't ever a tadpole might sound a little funny . . . but evolution creates the most unlikely creatures that flourish in their environments. And the smaller animals are, the more peculiar they can look to those of us looking in on their small worlds.

These impressive toads look even more amazing under ultraviolet light, which makes their fluorescent skeletons glow through their skin.

Life-size
AMPHIBIANS

Take a closer look at these tiny amphibians when they are drawn to actual size!

Small frog, big head!

Broad-snout casque-headed tree frog
LOCATED: Brazil
SIZE: 2.5 inches long
(snout-vent length)

Even though it's small, the olm is thought to be the largest cave animal in the world. In the past, some people believed they were baby dragons.

Olm
LOCATED: Southern Europe, particurlarly in Slovenia and Croatia
SIZE: 9.5 inches long
(head to tail end)

This small, slender salamander lives in underwater darkness

Taita Hills caecilian
LOCATED: Kenya
SIZE: 12 inches long
(head to tail end)

A little, legless amphibian with amazing adaptations

Oak toad
LOCATED: USA
SIZE: 0.8–1.2 inches long
(snout-vent length)

The smallest toad in the USA

The world's smallest vertebrate may be the **7–8mm** Brazilian flea toad (actually a frog), but new species are being discovered all the time.

Tiny and toxic

Pumpkin toadlet
LOCATED: Brazil
SIZE: 1 cm
(snout-vent length)

INVERTEBRATES

When most people think of an animal, they probably think about things with backbones—tigers and whales, lizards and snakes, frogs and toads, fishes and ducks. These animals are all vertebrates—things with backbones like a spine. But over 95% of all animals don't have backbones. Some might have strong armor covering their tiny bodies, but for the most part, life on Earth is *squishy*. These are the invertebrates, and they are everywhere!

Countless jellyfish coast the oceans through underwater clouds of krill, billions of almost microscopic worms and insects build the soil that the ground is made from, and swarms of insects pollinate the plants we depend on to grow our food. Not having bones means many of these animals can move in extraordinary patterns and behave in ways that might seem alien to humans, but they're just trying to do the same as other living creatures—find food, have babies, and not get eaten. Although giants like us might overlook the quadrillions of invertebrates that we share our planet with, their fascinating lives are always surprising when looked at under the microscope . . .

51

Monarch butterfly

Danaus plexippus

Across the length of North America, small, fragile darts of color skim over the leaves of forests and gardens. Whether crowding together in vast numbers in Mexico or coasting over the pines of New York state, monarchs are familiar, and to most humans, unremarkable butterflies. Until, that is, you take a closer look.

Coasting through the air at only 5.5 mph, a 3.5 inch-wide monarch butterfly could be a perfect, easily snatchable beak-full for any hungry bird. But monarchs have a secret weapon: when they are caterpillars, they eat milkweed. This small plant contains powerful toxins that are transferred into the insect's body as it eats, making both the caterpillar

Monarchs store three times as much of this foul-tasting poison in their wings than in their body, making sure that if a peckish predator snaps at a fluttering wing, it's likely the butterfly will be spat out before teeth or beak get to the less obvious body.

and its adult butterfly form a terrible taste for would-be predators.

Monarchs' bright wing patterns are examples of aposematic coloration. This means that although they make the butterflies easier to spot than if they were camouflaged, they warn predators such as black-headed grosbeaks that they taste bad, and it would be smart to stay away.

There might be another reason for the monarchs' patterned wings: some scientists think the white and darker spots help move heat around the surface of the wings, helping these butterflies save energy while flying through the air. Being tiny doesn't mean you're not mighty, and this toxic-winged, super-traveler is one of the hardiest insects around.

Flying as easily as possible is important because these tiny insects undertake extraordinary migrations each year. Every autumn, millions of the butterflies flap, tumble, and glide about 3,000 miles from their summer homes in the Northeastern US to Mexico. Then, as temperatures rise the following year, their offspring return up through North America, each generation continuing the journey.

Coconut octopus

Amphioctopus marginatus

The floor of the ocean around Bali, Sulawesi, and other Indonesian islands can be littered with trash—like coconut shells tossed into the ocean by careless humans. But instead of seeing trash on the shallow sea floor, a certain sneaky, 8 inch-long hunter sees opportunity.

Coconut octopuses earned their name because of the amazing way they use coconut shells. Scientists have spotted them picking up the discarded shells when they come across them on the lagoon floor, carrying them around, and then closing two halves together, hiding inside with just their eyes poking out. Then, when an unsuspecting crab walks nearby, the octopus shoots out and snatches a crunchy snack.

It's not just coconuts that these mollusks use to ambush their prey. They have been filmed using sea shells and other objects to create sneaky fortresses to pounce out of. And when there's nothing to find, they just hide under the lagoon's soft sand, completely undetectable.

Octopuses can move around by shooting water out of their hose-like siphon—like how air released from a balloon will make the balloon move in the opposite direction to the air—but they also *walk* on the ocean floor. Unlike almost all other octopuses, these miniature predators only use two of their arms when taking a stroll—leaving their other arms free to carry their tools of invisibility.

Octopus are smart. *Really* smart. In fact, some scientists think they might be as intelligent as some mammals, such as dogs or even certain primates. Finding objects to hide inside (and keeping them to use again) is a pretty clever trick. Discovering tool use in any animal species is spectacular, and it shocked scientists when they found it in an animal more closely related to a slug than to you or me.

Although coconut octopuses are soft-bodied (they don't have a skeleton), they are able to crunch, smash, and crack hard prey such as crabs, clams, and other shelled animals thanks to their horny beak, which lies in the center of their eight arms.

Common kingslayer
Malo kingi

Sometimes, it's the smallest animals that are the most dangerous. On the Australian mainland it pays to look out for spiders that can often inject powerful venom into fingers or toes. But that's on land. Off the coast of Queensland, the owner of one of the most powerful venoms in the world floats around the warm coastal waters amid surfers and scuba divers.

Common kingslayers are very small jellyfish. Their square bell (the dome-like part) is only 1 inch tall and almost impossible to spot: it's colorless and invisible in water. But from each corner of the bell, the kingslayer pulls lengthy thread-like tentacles up to three feet long behind it as it swims.

Its tentacles are covered in small, pale dots—the jellyfish's stingers (called nematocysts). When touched, these inject hugely painful venom that paralyses prey such as small fish, which are then pulled toward the bell and digested.

Kingslayers don't just float wherever the sea might take them. Like other box jellyfish, they have eyes with simple retinas and lenses (just like yours), so they can see where they would like to swim.

Together with a small number of other small species, kingslayers are known as Irukandji jellyfish, which all deliver venom so powerful they can be very harmful to humans. It makes their victims feel very scared of their surroundings, causing painful cramps, vomiting, heart attacks and even death.

Just because an animal is tiny doesn't necessarily mean it's harmless! Although most animals are more scared of humans than we should be of them, there are always exceptions to the rule.

Irukandji jellyfish are named after the Irukandji people, the Indigenous Australians who live in an area of Queensland where swimmers are occasionally stung.

Crabs usually use their claws to put food in their mouth, but pom-pom crabs have to use other legs to eat with instead, picking off tasty morsels from their tentacled protectors.

Pom-pom crab

Lybia edmondsoni

You never know where danger can lurk in a coral reef if you're tiny. The reefs around the islands of Hawaii are complicated mazes full of tunnels and crevices, pits and wells, all perfect for pairs of sharp, deadly jaws to be hiding in. But one 1 cm-wide crab has developed an unlikely defensive adaptation.

Pom-pom crabs (also called boxer crabs) have unusually small and weak claws (or chelea). But they don't need to use them for snapping—instead, they use them to hold onto two sea anemones. These flowery-looking jellyfish relatives pack a serious punch and sting when anything touches them. If any would-be predator approaches the crab—zap! A quick prod is all it takes to convince it that this invertebrate is definitely too painful to bother trying to eat.

Sea anemones can reproduce by splitting themselves in two, so if a crab ever loses one pom-pom, it can create another just by carefully tearing its remaining pom-pom in half.

Pom-pom crabs fight for the best patches of coral. But when they battle, they never use their anemones, instead holding them out of the way at the side of their bodies. Perhaps they are too important to get damaged!

Pom-pom crabs and their anemone friends are a great example of what scientists call mutualism: when two animals work together and both get something out of the deal. For the crab, the anemones provide protection from being eaten, but it's also a great arrangement for the anemone: it gets to be carried around to new exciting food sources much faster than it could move if it was living by itself.

Peacock spider
Maratus volans

Leaping forward with incredible bursts of speed, a metallic-blue and red speck hurtles over the sandy soil, dwarfed by the towering, thick grasses growing around it, swaying gently in a warm breeze. This peacock spider has its sights locked on a resting moth and won't stop its pursuit until it has delivered its fatal bite!

Spiders originally evolved to be ambush predators that wait and hide in crevices or ensnare unassuming insects in their sticky webs. But peacock spiders are "jumping" spiders: active predators that pursue their prey through miniature jungles. They may only be 5 mm long, but these are the hyaenas of the Australian undergrowth.

Peacock spiders target their prey using their sophisticated eyes. Not only do their huge front binocular eyes give them excellent 3-D vision for judging distances for jumping, but they can also see for long distances and even into the ultraviolet spectrum, seeing colors we humans can't.

Peacock spiders are impressive predators, but they also have a softer, more artistic side. When it's time to attract a mate, males unveil a beautiful multicolored fan that usually lies on top of their abdomen, kicking off a display of breathtaking grace and elegance.

Facing the female, the male sways his fan from side to side, while holding a pair of his white-socked legs outward and upward and occasionally stepping left and right. He vibrates his body, sending messages through the ground to the female. If all goes well, the female will let him mate with her—but if she's not impressed, he may end up as her lunch!

Peacock spiders are found in many habitats in Australia, but their intricate courtship rituals have only recently been discovered and studied by zoologists.

High speed chases and dramatic dances are just some of the amazing animal behaviors that occur all around us, but on a scale we humans aren't used to looking at.

Life-size
INVERTEBRATES

Take a closer look at these tiny invertebrates when they are drawn to actual size!

Monarch butterfly
LOCATED: USA, Canada, and Mexico
SIZE: 3.5-inch-wide wingspan

Miniature, master migrators

Small, sneaky, and smart!

The painted lady butterfly may have an even longer migration than that of the mighty monarch, making a **7,500 mile** round trip between Africa and Europe.

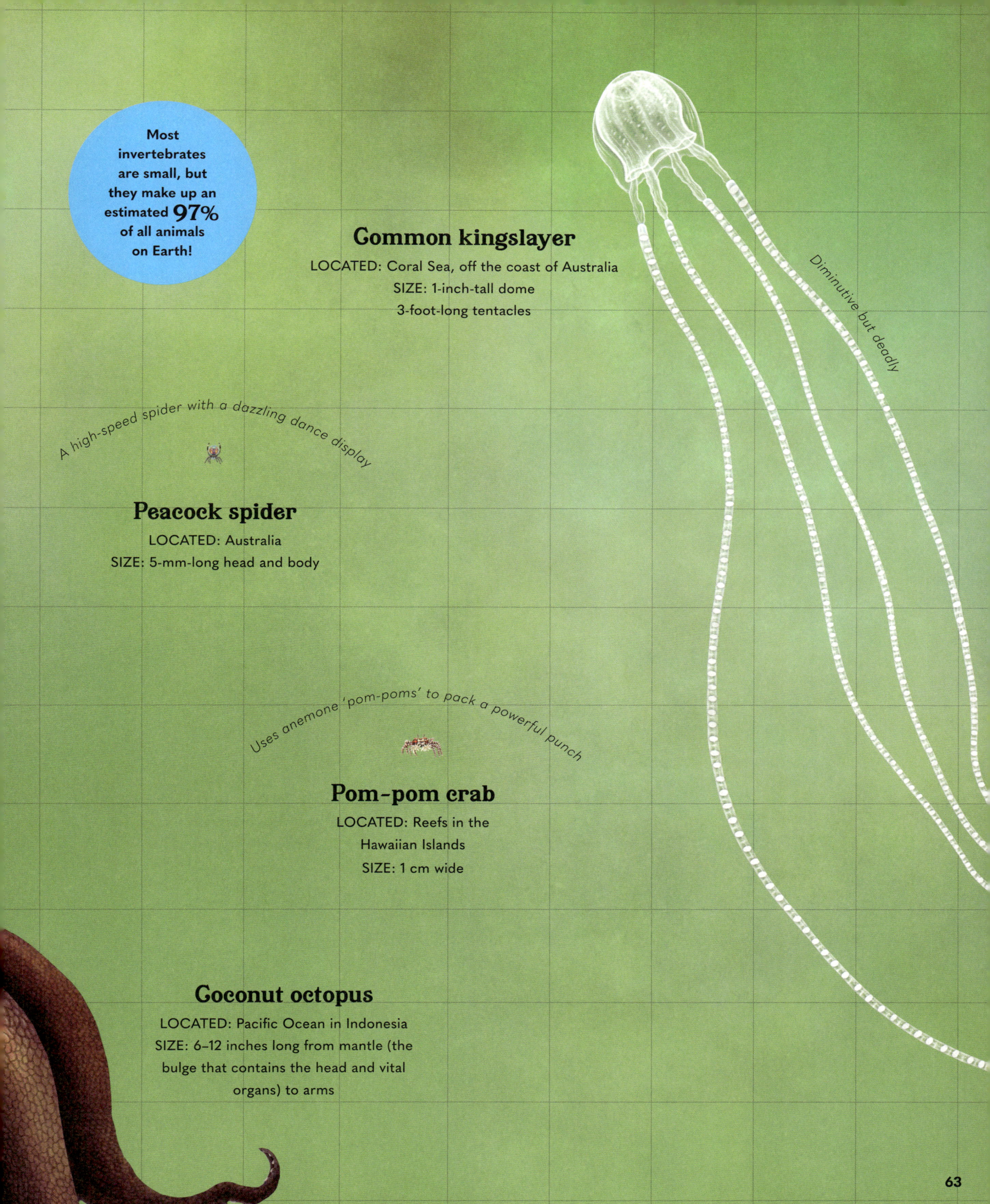

Most invertebrates are small, but they make up an estimated **97%** of all animals on Earth!

Common kingslayer
LOCATED: Coral Sea, off the coast of Australia
SIZE: 1-inch-tall dome
3-foot-long tentacles

Diminutive but deadly

A high-speed spider with a dazzling dance display

Peacock spider
LOCATED: Australia
SIZE: 5-mm-long head and body

Uses anemone 'pom-poms' to pack a powerful punch

Pom-pom crab
LOCATED: Reefs in the Hawaiian Islands
SIZE: 1 cm wide

Coconut octopus
LOCATED: Pacific Ocean in Indonesia
SIZE: 6–12 inches long from mantle (the bulge that contains the head and vital organs) to arms

MAMMALS

Everyone knows what mammals are—they're the group of fluffy, warm-blooded animals that humans belong to. Although most mammals, such as wolves, camels, pigs, and dolphins, are a fairly average size, mammals also happen to be the group that contains some of the biggest animals on Earth—like the gigantic blue whale. On the other end of the scale, there are also many very small mammals to be found rustling on forest floors or up in the canopy of trees in the dead of night, living secretive lives as they stuff their tiny bodies full of warming food. Both by specializing in particular foods (like bats, which hunt certain kinds of insects) or by eating whatever they can find (like foxes, which aren't picky in what they swipe), smaller mammals have become incredibly wide-ranging, and they are found on all continents on Earth as well as in all the surrounding oceans. But small mammals face the same challenges as their feathery and scaly relatives: they need to find food and avoid becoming food themselves, which can be difficult when they're the perfect size for a midnight snack.

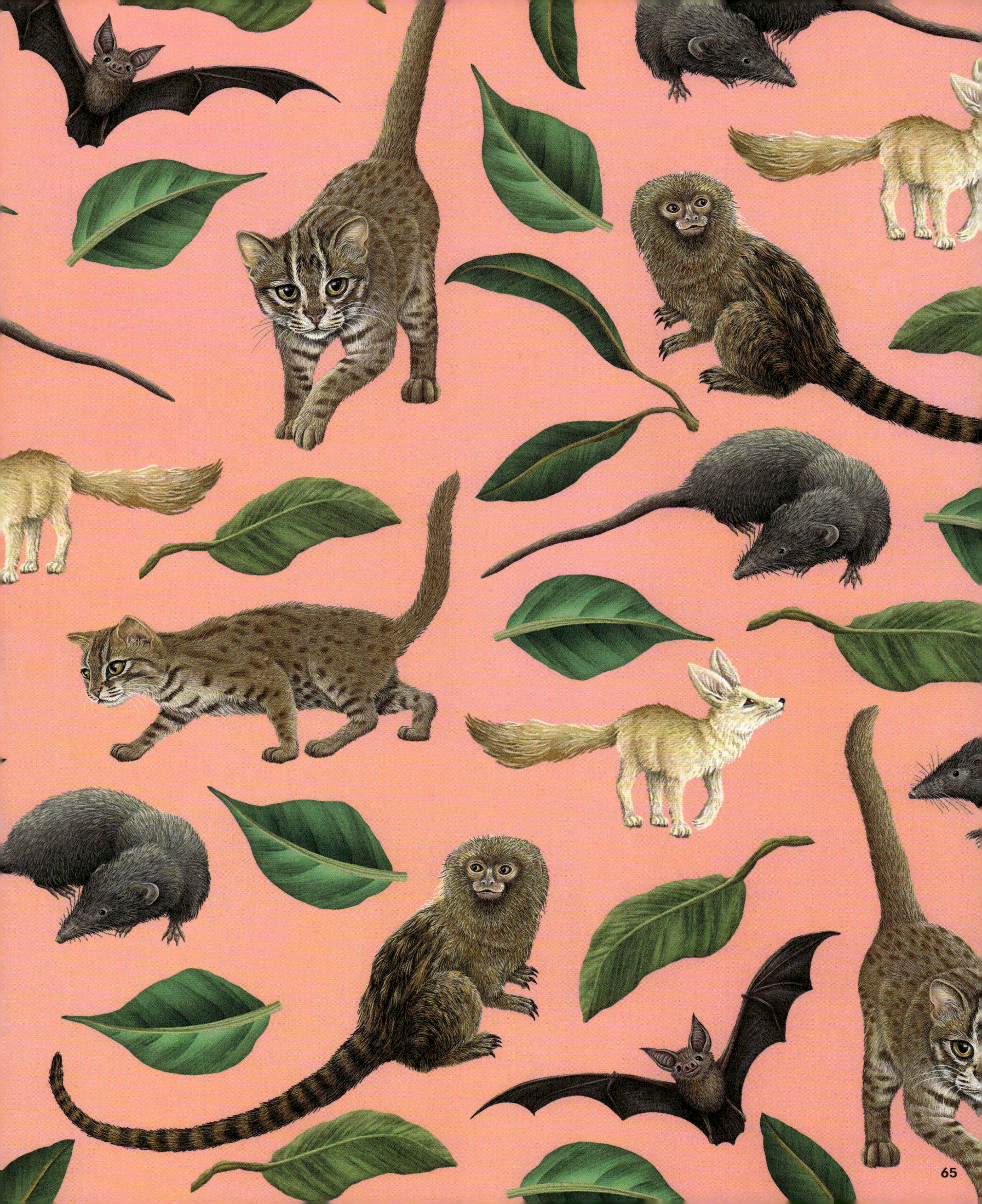

Hero shrew

Scutisorex somereni

In the tropical rainforest in the Congo Basin of Africa lives an unlikely hero. The 8 inch-long hero shrew is so named because of its almost unbelievable ability to survive being stepped on by animals—including humans—over 1,000 times as heavy as itself.

The secret of its heroic invincibility is this miniature mammal's spine. Unlike those of other shrews (and other mammals including humans) the hero shrew's spine has twice as many lower back bones as most other mammals, bends upward away from the ground, and each bone is enormously chunky, locking together with those in front and behind it. This forms a super-strong, shield-like barrier between its back and its soft internal organs.

Hero shrews spread a smelly scent from their fur onto the forest floor to warn other shrews to keep their distance. You might smell them, even if you don't see them . . .

What hero shrews actually use their incredible backbone for is still debated by zoologists. Recently, some have suggested that the shrew uses its back to push open and widen up gaps and cracks in logs and other parts of the undergrowth, like a lever, to reach worms and other insects it wouldn't otherwise be able to get to.

Unfortunately, no one has seen a hero shrew wedge open anything with its back, so at the moment this idea remains a "hypothesis"—a possibility that can be proved or disproved by a collection of data (like recording the shrew's behavior on a camera). Until then, the story behind this mini hero's superpower stays secret.

Kitti's hog-nosed bat

Craseonycteris thonglongyai

It is nearly dark above the waters of the Khwae Noi River in Thailand. The stars are starting to blink above the limestone banks, and clouds of insects are floating on the calm air. A soft, fluttering sound is beginning to drift out of the caves lining the river, and soon hundreds of insect-sized shadows flicker out of the caves' entrances, twisting upward over the river and along the banks. They are Kitti's hog-nosed bats (also known as bumblebee bats): at only 1 inch long, they are the smallest bat known to science, and one of the smallest mammals on Earth.

These reddish-brown bats are only found in a few places, like along the Khwae Noi River. Unlike a lot of other bat species, Kitti's hog-nosed bats like to keep lots of distance between themselves in their roosts, instead of crowding together.

After flying out of their roosts, the bats only search for prey for about 30 minutes, snatching tiny flies and grasshoppers from the dawn and dusk skies. Flapping wings up and down to stay in the air while chasing agile insects requires an enormous amount of energy.

The bat's wings are quite large in comparison to its minute body, and have extensions on their ends, which may mean that the bats hover during their hunts (possibly while snatching spiders and beetles off tree branches). However, scientists aren't sure exactly how they capture their food because the bats are difficult to follow.

The Kitti's hog-nosed bat was only described by Western scientists in 1974. It is named after Kitti Thonglongya, the Thai zoologist who discovered it.

Like all bats, the Kitti's hog-nosed bat is most reliant on its sense of hearing to navigate around its caves and locate prey in the sky. Although it has eyes, they are tiny and mostly covered by fur. Instead, it sees with sound, listening for the echoes from its ultrasonic calls to tell it where its prey is.

Fennec fox

Vulpes zerda

Padding softly and quickly on fluffy feet over the scalding sand of the Sahara Desert, a little fox is scouring the dunes for its next meal. There is no plant life apart from a few tufts of grass for miles around, which means there is no shade from the intensity of the Sun's heat. The temperature is almost 122°F, and there is no water for miles. But this is a fennec fox, and these tiny canids are true survivors.

Food is extremely hard to find in the desert, and so fennec foxes need to be able to notice anything that might be worth investigating. To do this, they rely on their enormous ears, which can hear even the smallest sounds—such as the scratches of insects or spiders beneath the sand—to their eardrums. Their enormous

Deserts are defined by their lack of water, and fennec foxes almost never come across puddles or rivers. Instead, their bodies extract all the water they need from their food.

ears also help the foxes lose heat. As their blood travels up into the thin ears, excess heat from their body gets transferred to their environment, cooling their bodies.

Being so small means Fennec foxes are very catchable snacks for raptors such as the Pharaoh eagle-owl.

Their beige-colored coat camouflages them against the sand, but the foxes also hide in vast, interconnected burrows, networks of tunnels under the sand. These subterranean fortresses also help them hide from the incredible heat of the day.

Fennec foxes only measure about 14 inches from their noses to the base of their tails. Being this small also helps them lose heat more quickly from their bodies than if they were bulkier (this is why animals that live in cold environments are usually larger than their relatives in hotter climates).

Because there isn't much food to find in the desert, fennec foxes aren't picky eaters, snacking on insects, small mammals like the greater Egyptian jerboa, and small lizards such as skinks.

Like other cats, the rusted spotted cat is an excellent climber and is able to pursue its prey up into the branches of the trees it hunts beneath. Being even smaller and lighter than domestic cats, they are able to chase prey into the canopy without the fear of breaking branches and plummeting to the ground.

Rusty-spotted cat

Prionailurus rubiginosus

It is nighttime in the Bardia National Park, Nepal, and through the dim, shadowy world that lies beneath the trees, a pair of large, searching eyes slip under leaves and over exposed roots. Smaller than a domestic cat, but looking a bit like a tabby, the rusty-spotted cat is the smallest species of cat on Earth.

As a felid (a member of the cat family), it hunts by stealth, moving extremely carefully and slowly to stay hidden until it is within striking distance of its prey, where it pounces with deadly speed.

Living and hunting in such hot climates as those in Nepal, India, and Sri Lanka,

Rusty-spotted cats only grow to around 14 inches, which makes them very difficult to find and study in the wild in and among the leafy forest floor. There is still much that is unknown about these tiny, elegant cats' behavior.

rusty-spotted cats have very short fur, which helps ensure they don't trap heat next to their skin, overheating their bodies. Although their brown and orange coloration might look obvious in a forest environment to humans, most mammals are red-green color-blind and can't see the difference between the rusty color of the cat's fur and the green forest. Instead, the black stripes and spots on its fur break up its outline and camouflage it under the dappled light of the forest.

Western pygmy marmoset

Cebuella pygmaea

Low hanging branches sway over the flooded forest floor of the northwest Amazon rainforest. Across these intertwining causeways speed golden-brown, tree-loving mammals, barely half as large as grey squirrels. But their tails aren't fluffy—they are slender, longer than the marmoset's bodies, and help them keep their balance. Not counting their tails, these western pygmy marmosets are only 5 inches long. They are some of the smallest monkeys on Earth.

It is a small troop—just a few individuals—made up of a single family. Each year, female pygmy marmosets give birth to twins, and older brothers and sisters take care of the new babies, which are only the size of golf balls when they are born!

Like other primates, western pygmy marmosets communicate with each other by making noises. Their voice boxes are too small to make hoots like larger monkeys. Instead, they make bird-like tweets and squeaks to reassure each other when they are close by, and slightly deeper sounds when they are calling across longer distances.

Trees are their homes but also their breakfast, lunch, and dinner: western pygmy marmosets live on a liquid diet of tree sap and gum. After scraping off a section of bark with their long front teeth, the marmosets lap up the sugar-rich sap the tree oozes to heal the wound. This troop will scrape over 100 holes in one tree before moving on to one of its neighbors.

Being small means these monkeys can use a food source other larger animals wouldn't find nourishing enough. But being small also means looking cute to humans, which can be a problem. Each year, thousands of pygmy marmosets are taken from their natural homes and sold to people as exotic pets, even though they become very unhappy in captivity.

Their hands are too small to grasp around the tree branches, so they rely on sharp claws at the ends of their fingers to grip the bark. Holding on like this, they can hang upside down, but can still look at the world right side up by twisting their necks 180 degrees.

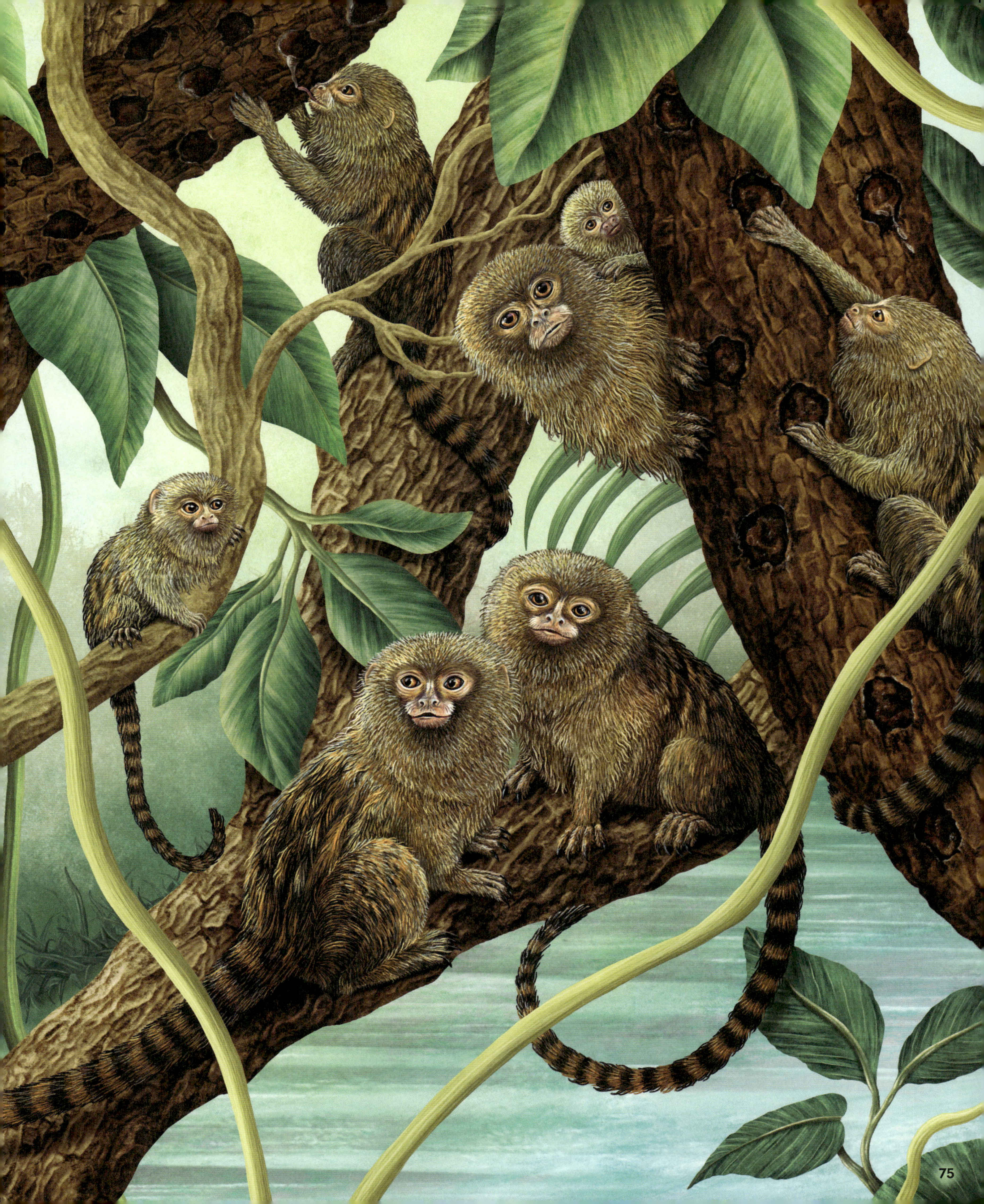

Life-size MAMMALS

Take a closer look at these tiny mammals when they are drawn to actual size!

Kitti's hog-nosed bat
LOCATED: Thailand and Myanmar
SIZE: 1 inch long

The world's smallest bat

Enormous ears help this little fox catch prey and stay cool

The fennec fox is the smallest member of the canid family, but its ears—which can be half the length of its body—are the largest, relative to body size.

Fennec fox
LOCATED: Sahara Desert and elsewhere in North Africa, including Morocco
SIZE: 14 inches long from nose to base of tail
7-inch-long tail

Hero shrew
LOCATED: Congo Basin
SIZE: 8 inches long from nose to tail end

This small superhero has a super-strong spine

Trees are home and food to these primates

Western pygmy marmoset
LOCATED: Amazon Basin
SIZE: 5 inches long from head to bottom
8-inch-long tail

The smallest cat

Rusty-spotted cat
LOCATED: India, Sri Lanka, and Nepal
SIZE: 14 inches long from nose to bottom
6-inch-long tail

REPTILES

Reptiles have been on planet Earth for longer than a lot of other types of animals, including birds and mammals, and throughout their long history, they have grown to be monstrous in size—such as the gargantuan titanosaurs that would dwarf a modern-day building—as well as incredible in their shapes—such as the humpbacked, claw-tailed drepanosaurs.

Today, some of the most fascinating reptiles aren't the giant monitor lizards or the armored crocodiles, but the smallest lizards, snakes, and turtles. Some of these animals have evolved incredible defenses to protect themselves from predators, while others have shrunk so small their bodies don't work in quite the same way as those of their larger relatives. But these pocket-sized evolutionary triumphs face another difficulty: humans can be tempted to keep some of these amazing species as pets—even when it can be very hard for them to survive away from their natural homes.

79

Nano-chameleon

Brookesia nana

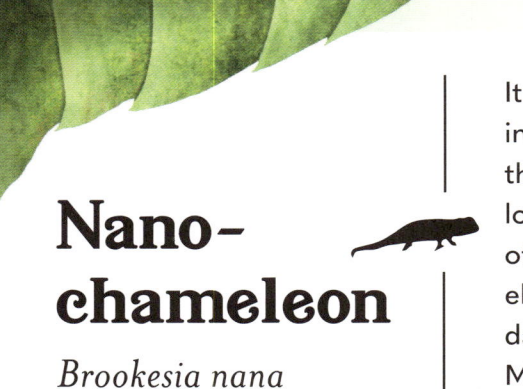

It is not unusual to discover chameleons in Madagascar. Overhead and underfoot, these color-changing, googly-eyed, long-tongued lizards abound. More species of chameleon live here than anywhere else on Earth. But look very closely at the damp forest floor around the Sorata Massif Mountains in the north of the island, and you may just be able to spot the smallest known reptile yet discovered: *Brookesia nano*—the nano-chameleon.

Including their tail, these lizards are tiny: females are *almost* 1 inch long and males only just stretch past 2 cm. Meandering across the forest floor rather than in the branches of trees like other chameleons, they hunt for tiny animals such as spiders, mites, and springtails, capturing them with their sticky, projectile tongues.

Nano-chameleons can't change color but being so small and colored a pale brown, they can easily use even short vegetation like grass to hide from nocturnal predators.

However, just because nano-chameleons don't change color and can't use their tails to hold on to branches, it doesn't mean they aren't as good at being chameleons. They can still capture prey, hide from predators, and move around their environment just the same as other, bigger chameleons . . . they just do things their own way!

Not living in the trees, nano-chameleons don't need to rely on their tails to help them grip branches. Instead, they use the tail like a fifth leg to help stabilize them as they walk across the uneven ground.

Armadillo lizard

Ouroborus cataphractus

The Karoo Desert in South Africa is one of the driest places on Earth—a dusty world where the largest plants to grow beneath thorny shrubs, and trees are tiny succulents, storing any water that they can find a few inches above the ground. Beneath their swollen leaves, a small lizard the same color as the rocks it hides between scampers out of its slim hiding places to look for food.

This brown and yellow pocket dragon is an armadillo lizard: only 10 inches long from its nose to the end of its scaly tail, and like the larger mammal it is named after, it depends on its tough scales for protection.

Despite their ferocious looking armor, armadillo lizards mainly eat small insects such as termites and beetles, along with other invertebrates such as millipedes.

Their armour protects them from bird of prey attacks, but they also rely on other armadillo lizards to keep a look-out for predators. They hang out in groups of up to sixty, each looking out for danger as they search for food under the blistering sunshine.

When it can't escape from trouble, an armadillo lizard can grab onto the end of its tail with its jaws to form a protective circle of scales, so no peckish predator can get at its softer underside. This ingenious defense gives armadillo lizards their scientific name: *Ouroborus*, an ancient symbol of an animal eating its own tail.

Although this is a smart way to protect yourself from predators, rolling up instead of running away is a bad idea if you're trying to stay safe from humans, since the lizards can easily (and illegally) be picked up and sold as pets.

Their thick, muscular tails also help the lizards communicate. By flicking the ends of their tails, they can send messages to one another about danger they might have spotted.

Speckled Cape tortoise

Chersobius signatus

Rocky outcrops are a great place to live if you're small. Just like armadillo lizards, this palm-sized vegetarian uses the cracks and crevices on the ground in South Africa's shrubland to hide itself away from predators. Measuring less than 4 inches long, speckled Cape tortoises are the world's smallest tortoises—teeny versions of their giant shelled cousins like the sheep-sized Galapagos tortoises.

Speckled Cape tortoises might look sweet, but they are quite aggressive and protect their small patches viciously from any unwelcome intruder. But fighting is worth it! Losing would mean a long voyage on little legs to find unclaimed territory.

Being small helps the tortoises to stay cool in the dry heat (the larger you are, the trickier it is to lose heat from your body). Another way they stay safe in this heat is to be active in the mornings, so they can enjoy cooler temperatures while they graze on the low-lying succulent plants.

Speckled Cape tortoises aren't easy to spot, but they can be tracked down by following the little paths they trample through the succulents. In fact, their name in the local Afrikaans language, "padloper," means "path-walker."

Unfortunately, humans can easily find the turtles by following these pathways and pick them up to be sold into captivity. This, combined with them being hunted by pigs and dogs and killed by traffic, means speckled Cape tortoises are not only the smallest tortoises, they are also one of the most endangered.

When danger is spotted but the tortoise can't reach a craggy hiding place in time, its spotted shell, called a carapace, keeps it camouflaged from the beady eyes of circling birds of prey.

Barbados threadsnake

Tetracheilostoma carlae

With white-sand beaches fringed by palm trees and sparkling shallow seas perfect for snorkelling around coral reefs, the Caribbean island of Barbados is a sensational summer vacation destination. But it's also a fascinating place to visit if you happen to be interested in herpetology (that is, if you're a fan of reptiles or amphibians). If your eyesight is good enough, you might even spot a very special reptile that, at first glance, might look a lot like a piece of burnt string on the forest floor . . .

The Barbados threadsnake is only 4 inches long, but it is a fully formed snake which,

Although tiny, Barbados threadsnakes are voracious predators. Their miniature bodies help them burrow into the soil and small cracks in wood, where they devour huge numbers of termites and ants.

despite having a body the same width as a piece of spaghetti, has all the body parts—ribs, eyeballs, and teeth—that you'd expect to find in a more usual-sized serpent.

To burrow through the ground, threadsnakes need a tough head to push soil out of the way. For this reason, the bones in threadsnakes' skulls are solid and fused together to make them very sturdy. This is unlike most other snakes' skulls, which are more loosely connected to help them open their mouths wide when swallowing food such as whole eggs and large animals.

Sitting in museum collections and incorrectly identified as another species, the Barbados threadsnake was only scientifically described by Western scientists in 2008 (although people from the island had known all about their little neighbor for a long time before that!).

Building eggs is a serious business and takes a lot of energy, especially when you're small. So, using the little energy it gets from its insect meals in the smartest possible way, the Barbados threadsnake grows only one egg (whereas other snakes lay tens or even hundreds of eggs when they breed). But their single egg is enormous, and their one hatchling emerges already half the length of its mother! Snakes probably can't physically be any smaller than this species and still be able to grow eggs.

Indian flying lizard

Draco dussumieri

High above the tangled roots and swinging vines of a tropical forest floor in Southern India, something skinny and scaly has spread its silvery-yellow wings and zips across the sky from one towering tree to another. But this is not a bird or a bat; it's a flying lizard, only around 8 inches from the tip of its snout to the end of its tail.

Flying lizards are sometimes called flying dragons, and that's what their scientific name means in Latin—*Draco*—but they don't actually fly, they glide. Instead of flapping wings, they coast on the air supported

By holding these sheets of skin (called patagia) out from their body with their arms, these insect-munching reptiles can soar for up to 98 feet after launching themselves into the air.

by two sheets of skin stretched out over extended rib bones on their sides.

Gliding from tree to tree is a brilliant way of getting around the jungle. Being this small makes these lizards a perfect-sized snack for tree snakes, kingfishers, and macaques, and when there are only a few branches to escape over, it's a huge help to be able to quickly and safely escape from one tree to another.

Flying lizards' first line of defense against predators is to avoid being noticed in the first place. Indian flying lizards are really well camouflaged; their grey-brown motley scales make them almost invisible against the tree bark they live on. But when males want to advertise how good looking they are to females, they flick out a bright yellow flag of skin on their throats (called a dewlap) to draw attention to themselves. They may be small, but they can send a big message.

Flying lizards aren't the only small animals to glide by holding out large, flat parts of their body. Species of squirrels, frogs, and even snakes have all evolved to glide this way to avoid predators and to seek out food on new trees. You never know what you might see if you look up!

Life-size REPTILES

Take a closer look at these tiny reptiles when they are drawn to actual size!

Armadillo lizard
LOCATED: South Africa
SIZE: 10 inches long from nose to tail end

Awesome adaptations help this little lizard protect itself

Most reptiles lay eggs, but the armadillo lizard is one of the few that gives birth to live young.

This diminutive "dragon" can glide a massive 98 feet

Indian flying lizard
LOCATED: India
SIZE: 8 inches long from tip of snout to tail end

The tiniest chameleon

Nano-chameleon
LOCATED: Madagascar
SIZE: 1 inch long from nose to tail end

Nano-chameleons were named after two were found by scientists in Madagascar in 2012. **95%** of the reptiles that live on this unique island are found nowhere else in the world.

Earth's tiniest tortoise uses its carapace for camouflage

Speckled Cape tortoise
LOCATED: South Africa
SIZE: 4-inch-long straight carapace length

The smallest snake in the world

Barbados threadsnake
LOCATED: Barbados
SIZE: 4 inches long

The very smallest ANIMALS

The animals we have met in this book are all small, and most of these small animals have a backbone: they are birds, amphibians, reptiles, fish, and mammals, otherwise called "vertebrates." But it is the invertebrates—those without any sort of hard, internal skeleton—that are the smallest animals of all. Not only are they astonishingly tiny and endlessly diverse, they are also all around us.

Nematodes

These smooth worms might not be as recognizable as their ringed relatives the earthworms, and at sizes from 2 mm down to 0.1 mm, they are much, much smaller. But their tiny size has made them hugely successful. There are over 25,000 species known to science (but there are probably close to one million species of them living on Earth) and they are thought to be one of the most numerous types of animals on the planet. These microscopic predators live by the tens of thousands in a single handful of soil, in deep sea trenches, at the tops of mountains, even 2 miles under Earth's surface! The world might look like it's run by humans, but scientists now think there are almost 60 billion nematodes for every single human being living on our planet.

Fairy wasps

The air around us is home to some of the most beautiful tiny creatures: fairy wasps. There are over 1,400 species of these insects, and they are all tiny—smaller than a single millimeter. Fairy wasps fly, but at this astonishing small size, air moves and feels more like a thick liquid than a gas, which the fairy wasps use their spindly, feather-like wings like paddles to wade through. One particular fairy wasp is *Kikiki huna*: at only 0.15mm long, it is the smallest flying insect ever discovered. The fairy wasps are all "parasitoids," animals that need to lay their eggs in other much larger insects in order for them to grow, eventually killing the animal they are laid inside of.

Zooplankton

Although the oceans are home to the most enormous animals on Earth, like the 98-foot-long blue whale and the 16.5-ton whale shark, they are also home to billions upon billions of tiny living things, many of which make up the diet of these huge filter feeders. Zooplankton, the animals that form part of this enormous group, are some of the tiniest creatures in the ocean. One of the most common types of zooplankton, which are pulled and pushed through the water by gigantic ocean currents, are the copepods. These 1–2 mm relatives of crabs and woodlice are, along with krill, one of the most numerous animals in the ocean, despite being barely visible to the naked eye.

Myxozoans

Nematodes are everywhere, fairy wasps paddle through the air, and copepods breed in such huge numbers they sustain Earth's largest predators. But the very smallest animals of all are a group scientists are only just slowly starting to understand. Myxozoans are cnidarians—members of the same family of animals that includes jellyfish and corals—but it wasn't until the early 21st century that scientists figured that out. Although some have the same stinging cells as their jellyfish relatives, myxozoans have incredibly simplified bodies: they don't have a nervous system or a gut, and many don't even have muscles, and none of them can live on their own. Instead, they live almost their entire lives inside the bodies of other animals, such as fish and frogs. Freed of so much body-baggage, myxozoans have shrunk down to truly microscopic sizes (the smallest myxozoans are only a hundredth of a mm long!) and some species' entire bodies are made of just one single cell, which is very, very unusual for an animal.

GLOSSARY

ADAPTATION
A new or different body part, shape or behavior that becomes more common across generations in a species, which helps them thrive in their environment.

AERIAL
Existing or happening in the air.

AFRIKAANS
An official language of South Africa.

AMPHIBIAN
An animal with a backbone that needs water for their young to grow. They tend to dry out in arid or hot environments. Frogs, toads, and salamanders are all amphibians.

BINOCULAR VISION
Using both eyes together to see one joined-up, three-dimensional image. Many predators, including birds of prey and lions, have binocular vision.

BIOLUMINESCENCE
The ability of living things to produce and emit light.

CAMOUFLAGE
The way in which some animals use colors, markings, or texture to help them blend in with their natural surroundings.

CAPTIVITY
Being kept confined in an enclosed space, instead of living in the wild.

CIRCULATORY SYSTEM
The network inside an animal that transports fluids, nutrients, oxygen, and some waste products around the body. In mammals, this includes the blood, arteries, veins, and the heart.

CONIFEROUS
Trees or shrubs that produce cones and grow in cooler parts of the world. Unlike deciduous plants like oak, rowan, and birch, almost all conifers do not shed their leaves every year.

COURTING RITUAL
A pattern of behavior displayed by an animal or a pair of animals together, when they are trying to attract a mate, such as dancing or making loud sounds.

CRUSTACEAN
An invertebrate with a hard covering (called an exoskeleton) and legs that split in two at their foot-ends, often living in water. Lobsters, crabs, and barnacles are all crustaceans.

ENDANGERED
A species that is at risk of going extinct.

EVOLUTION
The processes that lead to changes in a species' body and behavior that happen over long periods of time eventually leading to the origin of new species of living things.

EXOSKELETON
A hard outer covering that protects an animal's body, instead of having a skeleton on the inside (called an endoskeleton). Many invertebrates, including crabs and ants, have exoskeletons.

EXTINCTION
When the last member of a species dies.

FERAL
Animals living in the wild that previously lived in captivity.

FILAMENT
Whisker-like tendrils that extend from a creature, often used to sense movement of other living things nearby.

FLUORESCENCE
The way some surfaces give off visible, and sometimes colorful, light when they absorb certain types of other light, such as ultraviolet light.

INDIGENOUS
A term describing people, animals, or plants who are the original or earliest inhabitants of a place.

INVERTEBRATE
An animal that has no backbone. Most of the living creatures on Earth are invertebrates, including worms, jellyfish, and all kinds of insects.

IRIDESCENCE
The way some surfaces display many bright colors that seem to shimmer and change as the light moves on them, or if they are viewed from a different angle.

MAMMAL
A vertebrate that typically has fur or hair, three small bones in its ear, and produces milk (if female). Humans, whales, and kangaroos are all mammals. Almost all female mammals give birth to live young except platypuses and echidnas which lay soft eggs.

METAMORPHOSIS
A dramatic process by which an animal changes from a juvenile (young) form into a different adult form.

MIGRATION
The movement of animals, including mammals, birds, and fish, from one place to another at certain times of the year.

MOLLUSK
An invertebrate animal that has a soft body, and often, a hard shell to offer protection. Snails, oysters, and octopuses are all mollusks.

NERVOUS SYSTEM
The network inside an animal that sends messages between the body and the brain, resulting in reactions, movement, and other body functions.

NOCTURNAL
Being active at night. Most owls and bats are examples of nocturnal animals.

PARALYSIS
Not being able to move or feel all or some of your body.

PARASITE
An animal or plant that lives on or inside another living thing and feeds from it in order to stay alive.

PIGMENT
A substance that gives something color.

PLUMAGE
The feathers which cover the body of a bird.

PREDATOR
An animal that hunts, kills, and eats other animals.

PREY
An animal that is hunted, killed, and eaten by other animals.

PRIMATE
A member of the group of mammals that includes humans, apes, monkeys, and lemurs.

PROJECTILE
Being able to project or thrust a long way forward. Chameleons and frogs have projectile tongues that can be hurled from their mouths very quickly to catch prey.

SOUTHERN HEMISPHERE
The half of the Earth that lies south of the Equator.

SPECIES
The name for an individual type of living thing. Species are known by two-part scientific names (like '*Danaus plexippus*') as well as one or sometimes many 'common' names (like 'Monarch butterfly').

SUBTERRANEAN
Existing or happening below the ground.

TERRESTRIAL
Living on the ground instead of in the air, in water, or high up in trees.

TOXIN
A poisonous substance, sometimes produced by animals as a way of defending themselves against attack or used to weaken or kill prey.

TRANSPARENCY
When something allows light to pass through it, making it see-through.

ULTRASONIC
A type of sound wave that is so high pitched it is impossible for humans to hear. Animals including bats, dogs, and dolphins can hear ultrasonic sounds.

ULTRAVIOLET LIGHT
A type of light that is made up of shorter wavelengths than the light we can see, making it invisible to the human eye.

VENOM
A poison that is injected into another animal's body usually by biting or stinging. Venomous creatures include certain types of snakes, spiders, as well as some mammals.

VERTEBRATE
An animal that has a backbone. Birds, fish, amphibians, reptiles, and mammals, including humans, are all vertebrates.

ZOOLOGIST
A person who studies animals.

INDEX

Amazon, the 6, 74, 76
amphibians 36–49, 86, 92
Australia 18, 21, 56, 57, 60, 61, 63
Azores 30, 35

babies *see* young
Barbados 86, 87, 91
bioluminescence 29, 30
birds 8–21, 38, 52, 78, 82, 85, 92
Borneo 12, 34
Brazil 38, 46, 48, 49

camouflage 27, 39, 46, 53, 71, 73, 85, 89
caves 6, 36, 40, 68, 69
Colombia 28, 34
coloration 14, 18, 25, 26, 36, 42, 44, 46, 53, 61, 71, 73, 80, 81, 82
communication 28, 74, 83
coral reefs 26, 58, 86
Cuba 10

deserts 6, 70, 71, 82

eggs 11, 20, 28, 34, 36, 38, 39, 43, 46, 87, 91, 92
evolution 8, 43, 46, 78
extinction 18, 25

fish 22–35, 50, 56, 92, 93
forests 6, 14, 38, 39, 42, 44, 46, 52, 64, 66, 73, 74, 80, 86, 88

Hawaii 58, 63
hearing 14, 46, 69, 70
homes, animal 14, 25, 26, 27, 32, 39, 53, 74, 78
    burrows 18, 44, 71
    nests 11, 12, 16, 18, 21
    roosts 68

India 72, 88, 89, 91
Indonesia 21, 24, 26, 54
invertebrates 50–63, 82, 92–93

Kenya 42, 49

Lourie, Sara 27

Madagascar 80, 90
mammals 16, 54, 64–77, 78, 82, 92
mating 6, 11, 15, 18, 22, 28, 30, 31, 61
Mexico 20, 52, 53, 62
migrations 53, 62

Nepal 72, 77

oceans 6, 26, 28, 29, 30, 31, 32, 50, 54, 64, 93

parasitism 16, 31, 92
poisons *see* toxicity

reptiles 38, 78–91
rivers 6, 24, 68

sight 12, 13, 41, 60
smell 41, 45, 66
South Africa 82, 84
Sri Lanka 73
swamps 10

Tackett, Denise 27
taste 42, 45, 53
Thailand 68, 76
Thonglongya, Kitti 68
toxicity 32, 36, 42, 46, 52, 53, 56
trees 6, 8, 12, 14, 15, 22, 46, 64, 68, 70, 74, 81, 82, 86, 88, 89

USA 44, 49, 53, 62

venom *see* toxicity
vertebrates 24, 50, 92
vision *see* sight

young 6, 26, 28, 32, 38, 43, 91
    chicks 11, 16, 19
    tadpoles 39, 40, 46
    toadlets 46–47, 49